MEET THE PTERODACTYL

Fun Facts & Cool Pictures

Julian Hawking

Table of Contents

Meet the Pterodactyl

Pterodactyls are among the most famous of all ancient reptiles. Their wings make them look very different from other animals like them. They have captured the public's imagination ever since people found out about them. Even though pterodactyls lived a long time ago, scientists are learning more and more about them all the time. There are many different types of pterodactyls that are known today. Pterodactyls are part of a bigger group of winged reptiles called pterosaurs.

Pterodactyls were probably meat eaters that flew and hunted alone, although we don't know for sure. Part of the fun of studying animals that lived a long time ago is looking at their remains and trying to work backwards to learn about them. It's like detective work. One day, scientists will solve the 'case' of the pterodactyl!

Where Could You Find Pterodactyls and When?

Pterodactyls lived about 150 million years ago. This was during the Jurassic period, and it was in between the first and third big periods for dinosaurs and their relatives. Pterodactyls lived in areas that were probably very wet, like marshes that we have today.

During the Jurassic period, the pterosaurs ruled the sky. None of the modern flying creatures we know existed yet. There were lots of tropical forests all throughout the Jurassic period, which made a great environment for the pterodactyls. Scientists found the remains of pterodactyls in what is now Germany. They may have found some in Africa, too. The wet areas in those places made it easier for the pterodactyl bones to be preserved until they were found.

The Anatomy of Pterodactyls

Pterodactyls probably looked a little like bats and a little like birds—or at least the bats and birds we have today. Their wings were nearly three feet wide! Their fourth fingers were very long, and that's partly where they got their name, which means winged finger. The finger actually supports the wing of the pterodactyl.

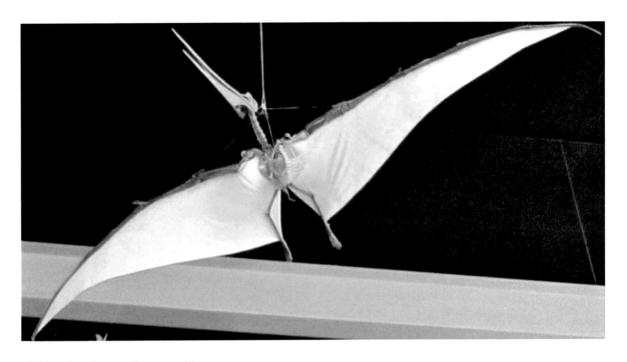

(Photo by ellenm1)

Many types of pterodactyls had long crests on the backs of their heads. The beaks of the pterodactyls were a lot longer than the beaks of many birds today. While birds have sharp beaks with no teeth, pterodactyls had sharp teeth like bats— and they had 90 of them!

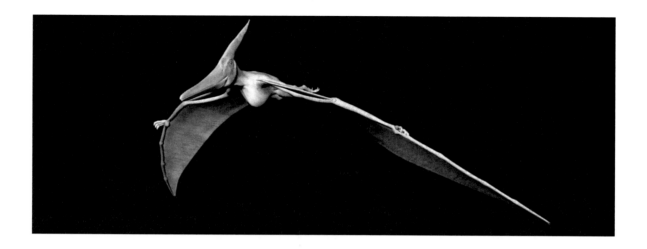

Scientists today are finding out that a lot of dinosaurs actually had feathers. They looked like feathered reptiles! One thing scientists don't know for sure is whether or not most pterodactyls had feathers. Some of them might have had feathers, but it was mostly the other dinosaurs that were feathered: they were more like birds than the reptiles with wings were!

How Did Pterodactyls Get Around?

Some birds have wings but don't use them to fly. Sometimes wings are just used for balance or swimming. Pterodactyls definitely used their wings to get around, hunt, and find other pterodactyls. They probably weren't very good at walking quickly!

Scientists can look at the wings of the pterodactyl and make an educated guess about how fast the pterodactyl could fly. Some scientists think pterodactyls used air currents to help them fly, like hawks.

Some birds today can walk, even though they wobble a lot from side to side and can't move very quickly. Pterodactyls probably had a slow speed on the ground. Their wings probably helped them balance whenever they had to walk on land, but they probably weren't very fast!

The World from the Perspective of a Pterodactyl

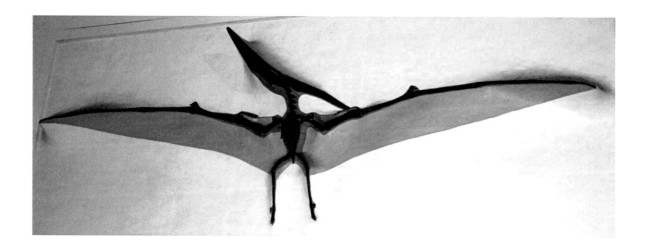

Pterodactyls may have had very good eyesight. Scientists can look at their skulls and figure out that some parts of their brains were very big, like the parts of the brain that help animals use their senses. Pterodactyls may have had powerful senses in general.

Lots of animals that have big wings will feel lots of things as they fly. They need to be able to understand everything that they are feeling. Pterodactyls were some of the biggest flying animals ever to have lived, so they may have needed great senses!

Pterodactyls probably had a good sense of touch. Lots of flying animals get around by paying close attention to sounds, too. When you change direction a lot during flight, using sound can be more important than sight.

Pterodactyls and Dinner

Scientists think that pterodactyls liked to eat fish. If you look at their beaks, they kind of look like pelican beaks, and pelicans eat fish. Animals with sharp teeth usually eat other animals, just like the pterodactyl did.

Pterodactyls may have eaten other types of little animals as well. They couldn't have eaten animals that were that much bigger than they were, though! Animals that eat really big animals usually have to hunt them together, and pterodactyls probably got their food by themselves most of the time.

Many animals that eat meat will eat dead animals if they have to or if they find them first. It's possible that when pterodactyls were hungry, they would scavenge for more food. Animals in the wild usually aren't picky eaters!

Pterodactyls with Other Pterodactyls

It can be hard for scientists to know a lot about how animals behaved when the animals lived a long time ago. Scientists can watch animals that live today living together right there in the wild, but with animals that lived a long time ago, like the pterodactyl, scientists sometimes have to make good guesses based on what they find.

Scientists have found pterodactyl eggs that make it look like pterodactyls might have been able to fly only a short while after they hatched! Since pterodactyls grew up so fast, they may not have spent much time with their parents.

Many pterodactyls did not fossilize together in groups. Scientists haven't always found big groups of them together, so it looks like they may not have stayed together until the end.

The Lives of Pterodactyls

Pterodactyls were probably awake during the day, unlike some of their cousins. The bones in the eye areas of their skulls make it appear as though pterodactyls didn't have the types of eyes animals need to get around at night. They didn't have flashlights, and they didn't glow in the dark, like some sea creatures!

Many other types of animals don't live as long as mammals. Scientists haven't found pterodactyls that seemed to have lived a long time. Pterodactyls may have lived for a few years— maybe a little more or a little less. They seem to have grown up very quickly, which can sometimes suggest that animals didn't live very long. Humans have long childhoods, and we live a long time!

Pterodactyl Fossils

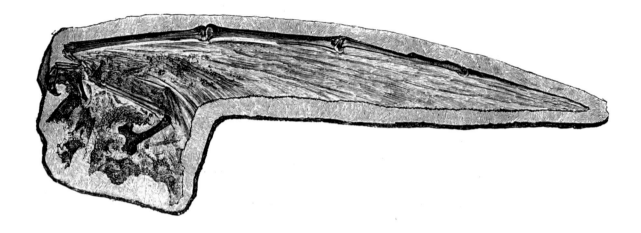

Scientists have learned almost everything they know about pterodactyls from the fossils they have found. Pterodactyl fossils were first found all the way back in the late 1700s, and many more have been found since then.

(Photo by Liné1)

There are all sorts of pterodactyl fossils that have been found to date. Scientists have pterodactyl teeth, pterodactyl skeletons, and imprints of pterodactyl skeletons. They have learned a lot from these pterodactyl bones.

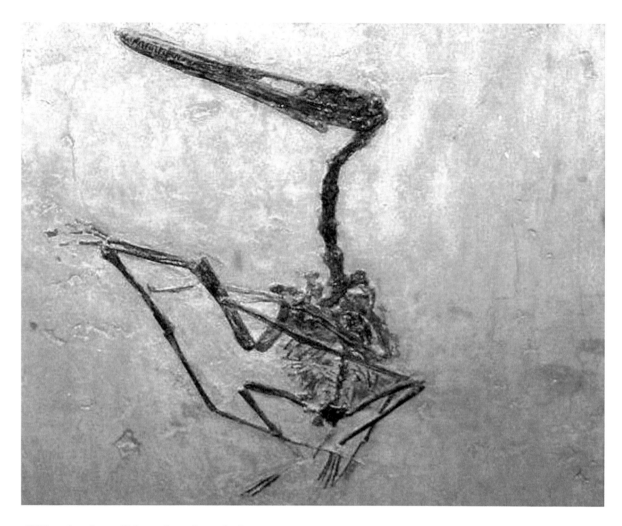

(Photo by Ghedoghedo)

Scientists will likely continue to find more and more pterodactyl fossils and learn more about pterosaurs as a group.

Weird Facts

Lots of scientists don't even think pterodactyls are dinosaurs at all! They lived with the dinosaurs, but they didn't move like them. Still, pterodactyls tend to be included in lineups of dinosaurs, and people will usually think of them that way.

Many people call all pterosaurs "pterodactyls." There are actually lots of different pterosaurs: the pterodactyl is only one kind. People get all the different kinds of pterosaurs mixed up all the time, and they've basically made up new animals in the process!

The skull crest on pterodactyls could have been used for all sorts of things; some scientists think that it helped pterodactyls with their flying. Whatever the skull crest was for, scientists don't understand it completely yet, even though the skull crest is so famous!

Pterodactyls and Stories

Lots of stories that include dinosaurs will also have pterodactyls. In a lot of those stories, people make the pterodactyls old-fashioned. Scientists have learned a lot about dinosaurs and their relatives since they have been studying them. Sometimes, the people who write stories don't read about the new things that scientists have learned, and so the characters they create look like they were written a long time ago.

Some famous dinosaur movies have pterodactyls. Usually, any big and flying reptile in a dinosaur movie is called a pterodactyl, even if it looks more like other kinds of pterosaurs. That happens a lot in dinosaur movies because of how long scientists have been learning about dinosaurs. Many long-necked dinosaurs in dinosaur movies are still called brontosauruses, even though scientists don't even use that word anymore!

Even though our knowledge has progressed rapidly, people haven't known about dinosaurs for that long, so most stories involving dinosaurs are new. People have known about other kinds of animals for so long that they've been featured in stories forever. Dinosaur and ancient reptile stories will always be new and modern, and they will keep getting even newer and more modern!

Other Books In This Series

Did you know that there are other dinosaur books in this series that you might enjoy?

Meet The T-Rex

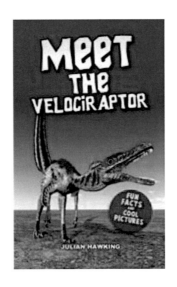

Meet The Velociraptor

Meet The Spinosaurus

Meet The Stegosaurus

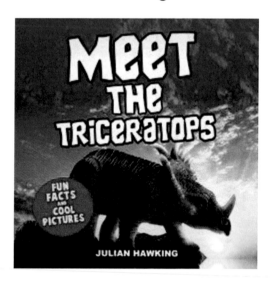

Meet The Triceratops

Meet The Brachiosaurus

Made in the USA
San Bernardino, CA
16 July 2015